WHO IS

The Hindu ~~~~~~~~~~

CHARACTERISTICS OF HINDUISM, FERTILITY
BABEL'S WORSHIP OF
THE HOST OF HEAVEN

From the Series: ***Strongholds & False Beliefs***
Doctrines of the World Order, the reign of Babel

Published by Torah Institute

ISBN: 9781495189869

1

By Lew White, educated by the Jesuit-Illuminati
Author's research spans 1983 to 2015
Copyright © 2015 by Lew White
Published by Torah Institute
POB 436044, Louisville, KY 40253 USA
502-261-9833
For more information visit
**fossilizedcustoms.com & torahzone.net
Amazon.com**
VISIT TORAH INSTITUTE'S YOUTUBE CHANNEL
On Facebook: Lew White, BYNV, & Torah Institute
TORAH INSTITUTE, POB 436044, LOUISVILLE, KY 40253-6044

CONTENTS

INTRODUCTION: JIHAD!

Jihad (dzihad): a word that applies to a range of ideas useful to express one's personal struggle, or exerted effort.

The **exoteric teaching** (for outsiders) of jihad is that of a spiritual, inner struggle or striving to change oneself.

The **esoteric teaching** (for insiders) of jihad is **warfare**. Economic warfare was shown to the world with the attack on the towers of the World Trade Center. Somalian pirates do the same by attacking ships, as was done in the early years of Islam in the Mediterranean Sea, and they continue to do so to this day.

Islam utilizes *everything* for warfare, even the womb. With up to 4 wives per man, any civilization can be overrun by population replacement alone (Bin Laden had 5 wives). Rape and murder of kafirs (unbelievers) is expected of adherents of Islam in the Quran and Hadith. There are too many verses of violence for anyone to believe they are all being misinterpreted.

The warfare is against all **kafirs** (non-Muslims), and inwardly against fellow Muslims of opposing sects: Shia against Sunni. The death toll of all this warfare over 1400 years is estimated to be in the area of 540 million. The fruit of this tree is destruction of all civilizations it encounters, and it is by far the fastest-growing "religion" in history. Islam means submission, and they are imposing that submission on all kafirs everywhere. It is not a state or political movement only; it is as if a **destroyer** has been unleashed upon all civilization bent on annihilation.

The thief seeks only to steal, kill, and destroy. Islamic hordes destroyed over 90% of the western world's libraries during its **golden age** (8th - 13th centuries).

The world they conquered around the Mediterranean Sea fell quickly, and it was ruled by Caliphates. Today we see cells of jihadists training over the Internet to kill and destroy nations from within. Government leaders claim *"we are not at war with Islam,"* and one even stated that ISIS is not driven by Islam. A week later another voice stated that one political candidate's will to block all Muslims from that country was fueling ISIS's recruitment and conversions to Islam. There is no such thing as a peaceful form of Islam. Radical Islam _is_ Islam, and it was all set in motion when a pope devised a plan to move from Rome to Jerusalem. Islam was invented by Catholicism, but that is another story.

Yahusha said, "**They shall put you out of the congregations, but an hour is coming when everyone who kills you shall think he is rendering service to Alahim.**" – Yn. 16:2
Religion has the uncanny ability to become a culture of death.

Here are some texts 1.6 billion people are taught to live by:
IS ISLAM A RELIGION OF PEACE, OR DESTRUCTION?
Quran 2:191: "Slay the unbelievers wherever you find them."
Quran 3:28: "Muslims must not take the infidels as friends."
Quran 3:85: "Maim and crucify the infidels if they criticize Islam."
Quran 8:12: "Terrorize and behead those who believe in scriptures other than the Quran."
Quran 8:60: "Muslims must muster all weapons to terrorize the infidels."
Quran 8:65: "The unbelievers are stupid; urge the Muslims to fight them."
Quran 9:5: "When opportunity arises, kill the infidels wherever you find them."
Quran 9:30: "The Jews and Christians are perverts, fight them."
Quran 9:123: "Make war (jihad) on the infidels living in your neighborhood."
Quran 22:19: "Punish the unbelievers with garments of fire, hooked iron rods, boiling water, melt their skin and bellies."
Quran 47:4: "Do not hanker for peace with the infidels; behead them when you catch them."

Islam emerged in the 7th century CE in the Middle East, centered at Mecca. An ancient shrine was already operating at this site, holding **360 deities** within its square room.
In practice, we notice remarkable similarities to Hinduism, such as the prayer beads, shrine with turrets, the crescent moon symbol, circumambulation around the shrine, and bowing toward the object of worship. There are diversions as well, the most striking aspect is how peaceful Hinduism is, contrasted with how violent Islam is. The traits of the Hindu deity Shiva (destroyer) involve violence and mutilation, the crescent moon, a black stone, beads (sometimes made from serpent vertebra) – closely relate to the most feared Indian deity: **Kali.**

THE KABA - HOUSE OF ALLAH
Previous address of 360 pagan deities, a cubic-shaped building called the Kaba (cube in Arabic) is the most sacred place on Earth to 1.6 billion devotees. They are obliged to make a pilgrimage there at least once in their lifetime.

WHAT WAS GOING ON AT MAKKAH
What did the people worship in Mecca prior to Muhammad's reformation? Who is Allah? Where is his house? Why do people walk around it? Is there a Hindu connection? The site of the Kaba was being used for some purpose that involved 360 pagan deities. The 360 deities hint at Babel's stellar religion.
The worship of the host of heaven infected the whole world, and the Far East received an enriched amount of Babel's religious behavior. As the stars rotate around the north star, Hindu shrines and temples were venerated by walking around them by the devotees. The 360 deities in the Kaba would logically not come about by random accident, but had spread there from elsewhere. The Babylonian worshippers of Nimrod, Semiramis, and Tammuz numbered the days at 360, linking their yearly cycle with the heavenly host. The three aspects of Hinduism are creation (Brahma), preservation (Vishnu), and destruction (Shiva). Is it possible the shrine at Makkah (Mecca) is an ancient Hindu site of Shiva worship? The symbol of Shiva is a crescent. All Muslims bow down and pray toward a building called the Kaba shrine. From what source comes the crescent?

Here is one of the earliest photographs of the site:

The square-shaped room above has one entrance, shown left of the center. **In recent decades it has grown to appear like this:**

THE BLACK STONE CONNECTION

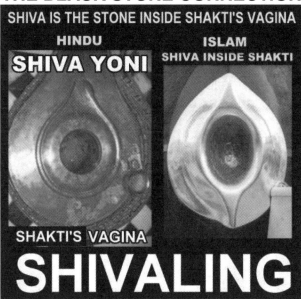

SHIVA IS THE STONE INSIDE SHAKTI'S VAGINA

HINDU — SHIVA YONI

ISLAM — SHIVA INSIDE SHAKTI

SHAKTI'S VAGINA

SHIVALING

The Black Stone of **Mecca**, or Kaaba Stone, is a Muslim relic. According to Islamic tradition, the stone dates back to the time of Adam and Eve. It is the eastern cornerstone of the Kaaba. **Considered sacred, the Black Stone is touched by pilgrims as they walk around the Kaba in the center of the Grand Mosque in Mecca, Saudi Arabia.** It is thought to be so sacred it can cure impotence, and any other disease for that matter.

Black Shiva Lingam Stone

Black Shiva Lingams are rare and considered very sacred. They are believed to contain energy for protection.

They were once only found in Hindu Temples. They're the source of the **New Age** idea that cosmic energies are present in crystals and various kinds of gems or stones.

The egg shape is considered a phallic symbol of the Hindu god Shiva. A shiva lingam represents both male and female, also thought of as the cosmic egg from which all creation emerged.

BLACK SHIVA LINGAM STONE

The *Shivaling* ritual is the most sacred in Hinduism. The stones may be any color, and are called **Shivalingams**. The egg-shaped stone is placed over the hole of the vagina-shaped metal object called a *yoni*, representing the vagina of Shiva's spouse **Shakti**. The egg-shaped stone and domes represent Shiva's phallus. The western world uses a **tree** and **wreath** as the occult sex objects for the nativity of the Sun. **In the Shivalingam ritual, milk is poured over the objects inside Shiva shrines like the ones pictured below:**

The cubical space above is the inside of a Shiva temple with the ritual objects (Shivalingams) on display.

With Shivalingams on display, pagan shrines were places where devotees worshipped the host of heaven by engaging in sexual activities, often in booths that encircled the shrine.
Shakti's object is shown below <u>without</u> the Shivalingam installed:

SHIVALING ON THE TEMPLE MOUNT?

As we see, pagan worship went underground, and meanings were hidden from the eyes of the casual observer. It's called "the occult" for a reason. The mystical meaning is understood only by those who receive the **esoteric** understanding. Those outside only see the surface, or **exoteric** understanding. From only what we've seen so far, there are shared objects and rituals found in Islam also used in and around the shrines of Hinduism.

One of them came before the other, borrowing the idolatry.

If we put everything together, something highly offensive to our Creator is going on literally in His face where He has placed His Name forever. The mosque on the Temple Mount is built with the features of a Shiva shrine, a huge Shivalingam and yoni united in the architecture, modelling a huge Shivalingam. Religious rituals and their objects hold occult meaning, but only to the initiated. To those outside, their minds are veiled to the inner meanings.

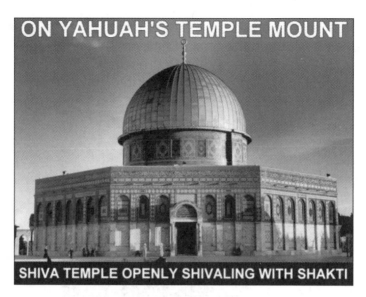

ON YAHUAH'S TEMPLE MOUNT

SHIVA TEMPLE OPENLY SHIVALING WITH SHAKTI

The domed object penetrating the central area of this structure has no significance to the worship of Yahuah, but a striking resemblance to Hinduism's worship of **Shiva** and **Shakti**.
The Far East is filled with Shiva shrines, many with central domes emerging from the center. There are two ritual objects associated with what is known as *shivaling*, and they are both on display in the architecture of many religious buildings.

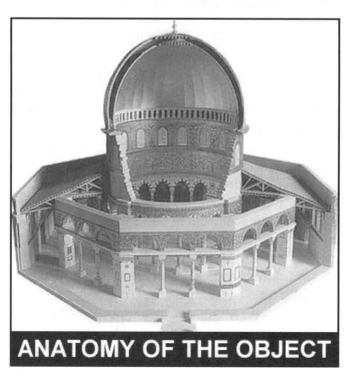

ANATOMY OF THE OBJECT

There's a **big stone** in the middle of the shrine. It believed to possibly be the foundation stone on which rested the Ark of the Covenant. Islamic tradition teaches it is a gift from Gabrial.
It is also believed to be the same stone on which Abram took his son Yitshaq to be offered to Yahuah on Mount Moriah.
For this reason it has Messianic significance.
The outrage of Yahuah will pour out on this Earth very soon.
He will shake not only the Earth, but also the heavens.
As we explore further in this short study, we will detect even more startling connections to Babel by way of Hinduism.

The population of Yeriko (Jericho) worshipped the Moon.
The name of the city itself refers to a Canaanite moon deity called Yarik, a word based on the Hebrew word for moon, **Yareah** (Strongs's H3394).
The worship of the host of heaven has spread everywhere from Babel. This overview simply points out some general connections one can easily make between Hinduism and Islamic architecture, objects, and rituals. This is only a snapshot.
The dome designs used all over the world in religious and governmental architecture also originate from the sexual symbolism of Shiva and the ritual called shivaling. The insertion of a black stone (shivalingam) into a yoni, then pouring milk over them, is the most sacred ritual performed in the Shiva shrine.

INSIDE ANOTHER SQUARE SHIVA SHRINE:

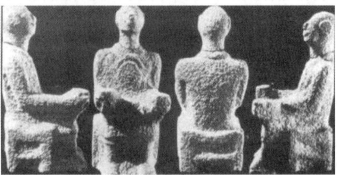

The moon-god from all four sides. Note the cresent moon carved on his chest.

Allah is represented by the object shown above from four different angles. The crescent is on its chest. The crescent and star in Hinduism represent Shiva and Shakti (see above).

CIRCUMAMBULATION

The ancient custom of *circular walking*, or circum-ambulating, is practiced by Hindus, Buddhists, Muslims, and Roman Catholics. Catholicism inherited many worship habits from Hinduism, such as ashes on foreheads, holy water (of the Ganges), haloes, images of deities, pillars on shrines, processions around shrines and cathedrals, and much more. Muhammad took 359 images of various deities out of the Kaba (cube), insisting there was only one deity, Allah. The kaba is considered the house of Allah, and Muslims practice the ancient custom of **walking around** it as an act of worship, just as they were accustomed to doing when the 360 idols were inside. This practice is called tawaf, and shows the worshiper's unity in their service to Allah. Wikipedia states:

"The circle begins from the Black Stone (al-Hajar al-'Aswad) on the corner of the Kaaba. If possible, Muslims are to kiss or touch it, but this is often not possible because of the large crowds, so it is acceptable for them to simply point or hold up their hand to the Stone on each circuit. They are also to make the Takbir prayer (Bismillah Allahu Akbar) each time they approach."

ISLAMIC METHOD (TOP) - HINDU & CATHOLIC (BELOW)

EGYPTIAN
MOON
DEITY

The Catholic "Mary" stands above on a crescent, an image shared from Babel, the Far East, Egypt, and many others.
The Babylonian trinity of Nimrod, Semiramis, and Tammuz became the model for all future pagan worship.
The worship of the **host of heaven**, focused on the babbled names of Nimrod as a Sun deity, is also called Astrology.
The Hindu trinity, Brahma, Vishnu, and Shiva (Sheba) show the principles of **creation**, **preservation**, and **destruction**. The third member of this trinity, Sheba, is associated consistently with the crescent moon, and the principle of **destruction**.

HINDU TRINITY

BRAHMA VISHNU SHEBA
CREATION - PRESERVATION - DESTRUCTION

SHEBA:
THE DESTROYER

CRESCENT
SERPENT
BEADS

SHEBA = ALLAH

14

PRAYER TO ALLAH, PRAYER TO MARY

I had read that Muslims pray to the mother of "Jesus" (whom they call **Isa**, from the Latin **IES** cryptonym seen in the Latin Vulgate as IESV).

In 1992, a Muslim came into the store I worked in and saw the dozens of postings all around teaching the Truth. He came up and asked me several questions, and I asked him one or two as well. I asked, **"How many beings do you pray to?"**
Immediately he answered, "One."
So I pressed him further**, "Do you also pray to Mary?"**
He then remembered that his faith also taught him to pray to Mary, but he did not know why.
I explained to him that Muslims pray to Mary because Catholics pray to her. He looked confused, and didn't know what to think.
The Quran mentions Mary 44 times, yet the Writings of Scripture only mention her name 19 times.
There is a shrine at Ephesus called the ***Ephesus Shrine***, and Muslims and Christians pray there daily together. Over 1 million devotees come there from all over the world to pray to Mary.

PRAYER BEADS

Originating in India, prayers to Shiva using beads began about the 8th century BCE (2800 years ago). Each prayer bead is related to a tear from Shiva's eye after a long meditation. The contruction of the device used seeds having five sides, connecting them to make a beaded mala, a bracelet and/or necklace. Shiva is often shown with both.

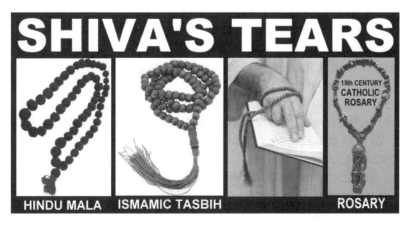

Hindu, Buddhist, Muslim, Catholic, Shinto, all share the repetitive prayer custom. Some also spin prayer wheels to send more prayers skyward in less time.

This practice began 2800 years ago in India, and passed into the Levant sometime during the Gnostic invasion from the Far East (beginning 200 BCE). Catholicism seems to have incorporated this Hindu device from several points. They refer to the beads as a chaplet, or rosary, meaning "rose garden."

Here's a photo of a 15th century Catholic rosary:

CATHOLIC SHIVA BEADS

The repetition of many prayers is not impressing Yahusha:
"And when praying, do not keep on babbling like the gentiles. For they think that they shall be heard for their many words. Therefore do not be like them, for your Father knows what you need before you ask Him." Mt. 6:7-8
It seems we do everything He told us not to do.

As followers of Yahusha, we understand we cannot do anything without being connected to our Root, because Yahusha is our Source of power to overcome whatever we wrestle against.
Our struggle is not against flesh and blood:
"For the rest, my brothers, be strong in the Master and in the mightiness of His strength. Put on the complete armor of Alahim, for you to have power to stand against the schemes of the devil.
Because we do not wrestle against flesh and blood, but against principalities, against authorities, against the world-rulers of the darkness of this age, against spiritual *matters* of wickedness in the heavenlies." Eph. 6:10-12
Unless we abide in Yahusha, we can do nothing. Yn. 15:5
We can attempt to do things without Yahusha, but we are engaged in spiritual warfare, and any fleshly effort exerted in such a war is absolutely futile in the extreme. Faulty teachings, human traditions, pagan customs, and doctrines of demons must

be overcome with the Truth, our sword, which is our offensive weapon to overthrow strongholds:

"For though we walk in the flesh, we do not fight according to the flesh. For the weapons we fight with are not fleshly but mighty in Alahim for overthrowing strongholds, overthrowing reasonings and every high matter that exalts itself against the knowledge of Alahim, taking captive every thought to make it obedient to the Mashiak, and being ready to punish all disobedience, when your obedience is complete." 2 Cor 10:3-6

The true character of Islam is found in the Quran. Its fruit is expressed in the outward display of brutality and massive destruction. It overtakes the weak by killing its enemies, and enslaving what is left.

Who is Allah? Almost one-fourth of this planet worships this deity. This amounts to about 1.6 billion people. They bow to a shrine located in Mecca (a Hebrew word, Makkah, meaning *slaughter, destruction*).

What was the former purpose of the shrine, and how does a Hindu symbol inform us of the identity of the deity?

 CRESCENT AND STAR SYMBOL

Islam developed as a monotheistic faith within the context of a polytheistic one. It inherited ritual objects such as the crescent and star from that polytheistic background. All pagan religions involved sexual elements in their "services," and their ritual objects portray this. Shiva and his consort Shakti play a highly sexual role in the religion of Hinduism. One of the most sacred ritual objects in Hinduism is the AUM (OM) symbol.

It represents the Hindu trinity of Brahma (creation), Vishnu (preservation), and Shiva (destruction). The crescent and star represent the sexual union of Shiva (crescent) and Shakti (star). **The ideas did not surface out of a vacuum at Makkah.** If the kaba is an ancient Shiva shrine, it explains why there is no ancient archaeological evidence of when it was originally built. It's original builders were definitely polytheistic. The kaba is only sacred to Islam because it was sacred to Muhammad. Almost one-fourth of this planet bows toward the *"house of Allah."* What was the former purpose of that shrine, and how does a **Hindu symbol** inform us of the identity of the deity?

Since the 8th century, a borderless spirit of war has been unleashed on this Earth. Historians recognize that gnostic ideas began to spread from the east beginning about 200 BCE. It was the old religion of Babel, and it was meshing with variations of itself. Babel's astrological symbols (zoo, or zodiac) spread everywhere. Hindu temples and mosques are the same things, but one focuses on the worship of **the destroyer:** Hebrew: **Abaddon**, Greek: **Apollyon**

The *Tower of Babel* design is expressed in the stupas, steeples, spires, obelisks, and minarets (as seen around mosques). Gold balls (Suns) are commonly part of the design, also widely used on flag poles, May poles (asherim), steeples, obelisks, and minarets.

Babel's astrology was the worship of the **host of heaven.** The worship services employed shrine prostitutes (nuns, mamakunas) since **fertility** was the base objective. The sex drive was harnessed by the dragon to achieve control over mankind. We see the power of this sexual enticement working at Numbers 25:1-3, as Yahuah's people joined to **Baal Peor** by committing whoredom with the women of Moab. (see Rev. 2:14) A typical pagan temple was surrounded by booths with straw floors where the "worship services" were performed.

Enslaved temple prostitutes **covered themselves** to remain anonymous. Yahudah's daughter-in-law Tamar **covered herself** at Genesis 38:19. Sitting beside the road to a pagan shrine, she deceived Yahudah to make him believe she was a shrine prostitute. The purpose of the burqa was primarily for the anonymity of prostitutes. The only connection it has with ritual religion is that of pagan temple prostitutes.

Yahuah has made no instruction in the use of a burqa.

Since the confusion of languages at the Tower of Babel, the dragon has ruled the hearts of all nations through astrology's occult mysteries. What has been hidden is now being revealed to be the Mother of Harlots: Babel the great. We wrestle against forces in the heavenlies, their doctrines of demons.

The folded hands (Namaste) is a Hindu/Buddhist gesture of worshipping forces. Snakes, crescents, beads, bowing, circular walking, praying in circles, are not of Yahuah.

The Arabic language gives us insight into the **phonology** of original Hebrew. These two languages are very closely related, as are the people speaking the languages. One group was chosen by Yahuah in a Covenant of love to draw all mankind to Himself in love. *The other followed another path:*
"And the Messenger of Yahuah said to her, 'See, you are

conceiving and bearing a son, and shall call his name
Yishmaal, because Yahuah has heard your affliction.
And he is to be a wild man, his hand against every one and
every one's hand against him, and dwell over against all his
brothers." - Gen. 16:11-12

WE ARE TO AVOID PAGAN CUSTOMS

"And now, fear Yahuah, serve Him in perfection and in truth,
and put away the mighty ones which your fathers served
beyond the River and in Mitsrayim, and serve Yahuah!
And if it seems evil in your eyes to serve Yahuah choose for
yourselves this day whom you are going to serve, whether
the mighty ones which your fathers served that were
beyond the River, or the mighty ones of the Amorites, in
whose land you dwell. But I and my house, we serve
Yahuah." - Yahusha/Joshua 24:14-15

ALAH - THE HEBREW ORIGIN OF THE WORD

There is confusion about the term **ALAH** (alef-lamed-hay)
because it is mistaken to be a proper noun, or name of a deity.
Alah is a Hebrew term, and is **not a name**. Alah is the pronoun
the Muslims call an ancient moon deity.

Al, Alah, and Alahim (aka ELAH) are pronouns understood to
mean **the god.** The root **AL** is spelled alef-lamed meaning
upwardness, exalted, mighty, high, above, etc.,.

The language of the descendants of Yishmaal is very close to
that of their father, Abrahim. The **crescent moon** symbol has
been taken to symbolize a faith group called **Islam** since the 7th
century. Worshipping things in **"the heavens above"** is
prohibited by the 2nd Commandment.

We should never bow-down to any images.

The **worship of the host of heaven** (zodiac, constellations) has
always been a stumbling-block for the nations.

The symbol of a **crescent Moon** shown beneath the Sun is a
common image used throughout history.

In plain sight on the US Great Seal, the lower banner forms
a **crescent**. The nations bowed to symbols of their deities, and
referred to them in coded, secret terminology. They would not
openly use the name of their deity. The nations inherited their
patterns of behavior from Babel's **worship of the host of
heaven**. (See book, Nimrod's Secret Identity) The **crescent
moon symbol** is the prominent image for the Islamic faith.
Adherents are trained to bow to a building in Mecca (Makkah,
meaning destruction or slaughter in Hebrew) containing images

of the host of heaven. These have sexual symbolism associated with them. Babel's fertility practices have filled the planet with idolatry.

THE LANGUAGE OF ABRAHIM

Arabs retain a much more accurate phonology of Hebrew (the language of Eber and Abrahim) because they've always spoken it. They were never scattered into the nations to corrupt their speech. They name their children proper Hebrew names like **Danial, Yusef, Yakub, Tamar, Zara, Ashah, Aliyah, Aquila, Daud**, and dozens more. They preserve the Hebrew name **Ali,** which was distorted slightly by the Masorete's vowels. Today it is commonly seen as **Eli.**

Their spiritual practices and customs are highly idolatrous. Any bowing to images is an abomination. The moon deity of Muhammad's clan was highly preferred. He claimed Allah was "the greatest." The term **alah** may refer to any deity, it is not a proper noun (a name). It's still a clean Hebrew word, spelled ALEF-LAMED-HAY. It is found more often in the **book of Danial** than any other place in Scripture.

Their **alah** (god) is not our **Alah** (God).

We should know that the term "God" originates as a pagan term, in fact a name for the **Sun**. It was adopted from Teutonic pagans by Christianity and applied to the Supreme Being. The 1945 Encyclopedia Americana has this to say under to topic **GOD:**

"GOD (god) **Common Teutonic word for personal object of religious worship, formerly applicable to super-human beings of heathen myth; on conversion of Teutonic races to Christianity, term was applied to Supreme Being."**

The first super-human ever worshipped was Nimrod, Babel's Great Architect, the builder of the Tower.

We should not use the term "god" because of its origin; but we may restore the Hebrew term **alah** to our speech. The term has nothing to do with Islam, the Moon, crescents, or kneeling face down on a mat facing Makkah.

Who is Allah?
Why do people walk around his shrine?

Walking around venerated objects comes from Hinduism. Yahuah Alahim is not Allah the moon deity of the Kaba

The Kaba is called the *house of Allah*.

Muslims know the term *Allah* is not a name, but a pronoun meaning "*the god*." But on the other hand, they believe their deity has 99 names. This is one of the traits of Hindusim, since there are trinities upon trinities, upon trinities. First let's learn a little more about the Hebrew origin of the word *alah.* Restoring the letter **A** to Alahim (seen as Elohim) does not associate the word *(alef-lamed-hay)* with *Islam*, although that may be a normal person's initial reaction.

Next, let's consider some letters:

In the 8th century, a new sect called **Karaites** (aka Masoretes) altered the *sound* of the letter **alef** (A) to **ayin** (E) using *niqqud* markings they had invented to **bend** the pronunciation of vowels. This sect began with **Anan Ben David** in 767, who also adopted the *sighted moon* (crescent-sighting) of the Muslims while under a Muslim Caliphate in the city of Babylon. In 767 Anan was imprisoned to be executed for rebellion, but the Islamic Caliph in Babylon spared his life because he distinguished himself from his Yahidim brethren **by adopting the sighted-moon** of the Muslims. This new sect, the **Masoretes** *(traditionalists)* did not want anyone to properly speak the four vowels of the Name **YOD-HAY-UAU-HAY** (Yahuah), so they invented *vowel distortions* using niqqud and cantillation marks to re-train readers of Hebrew to *mispronounce certain words.*

ALAHIM became **ELOHIM**, and **YAHU** became **YEHO**.

They left the name ***ABRAHIM*** alone, otherwise it would be called ***EBRAHIM*** by everyone today. The Hebrew root ***AL*** (alef-lamed) became ***EL***. This root is not a name, it is a pronoun referring to one who is **lofty**, **upward**, **above**, **high**, **strong**, **mighty**, etc.,. Israel's airline is ***EL-AL,*** and means "to go upward."

EL-AL is spelled ***ayin***-*lamed* (EL) + ***alef***-*lamed* (AL).

Yahuah Alahim means: *"I AM (your) MIGHTY ONE."*

Their Allah is not our Yahuah. We do not bow down to objects representing the host of heaven. It's idolatry. Ritual objects formerly and currently used to worship pagan deities are found everywhere in open view of everyone. They are veiled to the minds of those who only see the exoteric meaning.

DOME AT ROME: HINDU SHIVA SHRINE

EGYPTIAN OBELISK IN THE OVATO TONDO - HINDU WHEEL OF LIFE

The shape of the oval space above mimmicks the shape of the Hindu ritual object called the yoni (Shakti) into which the male object (Shiva) is inserted.

The Egyptian stone obelisk completes the Shivalingam.

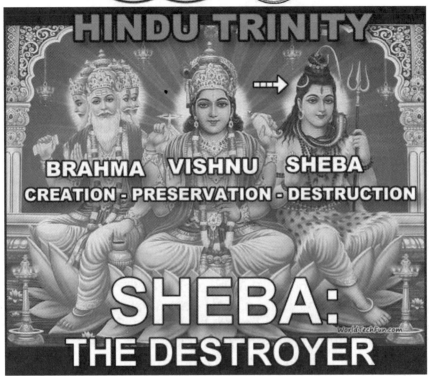

TRINITARIAN ORIGINS: BABEL

The triangle and triquetra in religious imagery represents the principles of *creation, preservation, and destruction.* Babel's Trinity, Nimrod, Semiramis, and Tammuz are reflected in the Hindu trinity of Brahma, Vishnu, and Shiva. A better rendering for Shiva is *Sheba.* We will use the spelling *Shiva* since it is not exactly right, and because there was no letter "V" as we use it today. Shiva is the babbled name for Tammuz, the reincarnation of Nimrod, the great architect of star-worship, and the originator of Babel the Great, the **Mother of Harlots**.

BLUE SKIN?

The blue skin of the Hindu deities represented their ascended state, taking on the color of the sky.

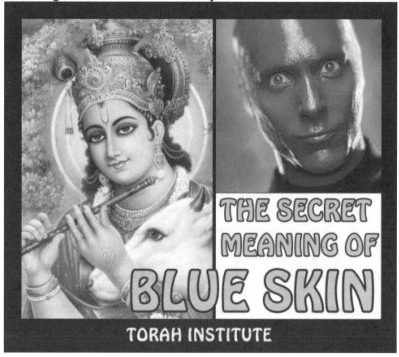

Amun, Re, and Ptah became the Egyptian triad. Sumeria's astrology, the worship of the host of heaven, was inherited by every culture. Trinities, fertility symbols, human sacrifices, reincarnation, and much more leaven spread Babel's idolatry far and wide.

ORIGIN OF REINCARNATION

The cycle of "rebirth" (reincarnation) originates from Babel's trinity, Nimrod, Semiramis, and Tammuz. After their king Nimrod was slain, their mythology taught that he ascended high into the heavens to become the Sun. Nimrod's wife Semiramis was found to carry his child, having been impregnated by the rays of the Sun. Tammuz was born as Nimrod *reincarnated*. In this way Semiramis was Nimrod's wife as well as his mother!

We serve only Yahuah, the Maker of heaven and earth. Pagans worship in the ways of Nimrod, Semiramis, and Tammuz, the first beast. The re-born Sun was Nimrod. The Hindu trinity reveals Allah to be the same as Shiva, *the destroyer*. The Kaba is the original site of a sex temple. The ancient Hindu shrine is still in operation, complete with worshippers doing everything demanded, including circumambulation, circular walking around an object of worship.

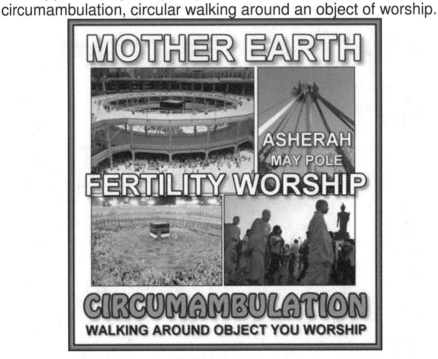

IT'S LIKE THE SEVENTH CENTURY ALL THE TIME

Up until the time of Mohammad, the Arabs worshipped hundreds of deities. The big black cube called the **Kaba** (Arabic for **cube**) was filled with 360 images of their deities, one of which was called Allah - a **moon deity**.

YEARLY ISLAMIC PRACTICE: DAY OF ASHURA

The origin of this practice, again, comes from Hinduism's gods. Wikipedia describes the character of these demonic demigods: **"The state of an Asura reflects the mental state of a human being obsessed with ego, force and violence, always looking for an excuse to get into a fight, angry with**

everyone and unable to maintain calm or solve problems peacefully." These demons meditated on war.

The Japanese pronunciation of these evil Hindu demons is Ashura, and the origin is Hinduism. The Japanese celebrate Ashura as their god of battle. To Muslims, the **Day of Ashura** pertains to fasting, mourning, and the remembrance of a massacre, and has differences depending on whether one is Shia or Sunni. The word **Asherah** is likely related to the term, a wooden object erected for worship very much like a Maypole.

A corner of the Kaba has a black touchstone with a vagina-shaped object representing Shakti's vagina, and Shiva (the black stone) is stuffed into it. Tradition has altered the names.

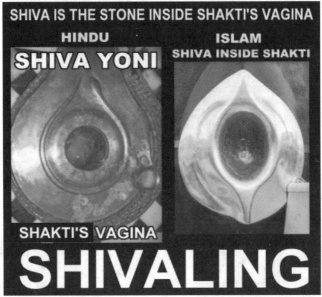

SHIVA IS THE STONE INSIDE SHAKTI'S VAGINA

HINDU — ISLAM

SHIVA YONI — SHIVA INSIDE SHAKTI

SHAKTI'S VAGINA

SHIVALING

Babel's *mother goddess* is in this. **Asherah** was the moon deity of the kananites, and Yericho was a major seat of her devotees. The Hindu deity **Shakti** is the same as Asherah, Baal's consort. **Shiva** and **Allah** are essentially the same deity. Muhammad declared Allah to be the greatest (of the deities). The **moon symbol** is prominent in this religion. Islam means *submission*. Muhammad was born in the midst of the pagan Arabs, and his clan watched over the Kaba, a square shaped building. Inside the cube were 360 idols worshipped by means of cult prostitutes who serviced those who made pilgrimages to Mecca.

They would **circumambulate** (walk around) the cubical building, just as the Hindus circumambulate around their Shiva temples and other shrines called **stupas**.

The **May Pole** custom exhibits fertility in a similar way, using virginal girls holding **ribbons** (hymen symbols) to rotate a wreath (vagina) downward on a **wooden pole** (asherah).

Yahuah hates these fertility practices. He calls it witchcraft.

PALESTINIAN: LATINIZED FROM PHILISTINE
Abrahim and the Egyptian servant of Sarah, Hagar, produced Yishmaal, the first-born. Sometime later Sarah began to deal harshly with Hagar, and Sarah departed with Yishmaal. Yahuah intervened, and sent Hagar back.
He told Hagar what Yishmaal would be like:
"And he will be a wild man; his hand *will be* against every man, and every man's hand against him; and he shall dwell in the presence of all his brethren." – Gen. 16:12

Yishmaalites and Yisharalites are both Hebrews, and are brothers, yet they fight over the land given to Abrahim's seed. Their main point of conflict is who they worship. The two sects of Islam, Sunni and Shia, have been fighting from the beginning. The Romans conquered Yahudah and destroyed the Temple in 70 CE. Vespasian named the land *Palestine*, a Latinism for **Philistia** (the former site of the *Philistines*) a region that was visited by Abrahim. If Arabs refer to themselves as **Palestinians**, they label themselves *Philistines*. They do this making it seem their claim to the land pre-dates the tribes of Yisharal.
Genesis 21:34 states *"Abrahim sojourned in the land of the Philistines many days."* Obviously, Abrahim wasn't a Philistine, so neither were his sons **Yitshaq** and **Yishmaal**. Yishmaal was half Egyptian, because Hagar was Egyptian. Yishmaal means

"Alahim hears." Arabs are children of Abrahim (a Hebrew), and are not the children of the Philistines. The fruit (behavior) of a faith shows what kind of tree it is, either good or bad.

Many crescent symbols are found among pagan religions.

ROMAN COINAGE

Muslims know the term **Allah** is not a name, but a pronoun meaning **the god**.

The Hebrew word **ALAH** *(alef-lamed-hay)* is not associated with **Islam**, although that may be the first reaction when we see the spelling "alah" rather than the traditional "elah."

The Pharisees did not twist the letter alef (A) into ayin (E), it was twisted by a Karaite sect called the **Masoretes**. This sect began with Anan Ben David in 767 adopting the **sighted-moon** (crescent-sighting) of the Muslims. The Islamic Caliph in Babylon spared his life because he adopted this method.

This sect of Masoretes (traditionalists) did not want anyone uttering the true Name YOD-HAY-UAU-HAY as "Yahuah," so they invented vowel distortions with niqqud and cantillation marks to train those reading Hebrew to mispronounce words. ALAHIM (or ALAHYM) became "ELOHIM."

YAHU became YEHO. They left the name ABRAHIM alone, otherwise it would be EBRAHIM today.

The Hebrew root "AL" (ALEF-LAMED) became "EL."

This root is not a name of any kind, it is a pronoun implying lofty, upward, highness, strength, mightiness, etc. The airline EL-AL means *to go* + *upward*.

EL-AL is spelled *ayin-lamed* (EL) + *alef-lamed* (AL).

NOTE CRESCENT SYMBOL

SHEBA = ALLAH

In Hinduism, ascended beings are represented with **blue skin** to associate them with the **blue sky**. Sheba the destroyer is shown above with prayer beads, a serpent, ashes on the forehead, a third eye, the AUM symbol, and crescent and star.

The crescent and star symbol has sexual meaning that is part of Hinduism's three principles of creation, sustenance, and destruction. The crescent and star represent **Shiva** and his spouse **Shakti** performing what is called *Shivaling*. The more we learn about what these occult symbols mean, the more we comprehend why Yahuah called these practices **"abominations of the Earth."** The meanings are withheld from the masses.

We do not bow down to symbols or objects representing the host of heaven. Many cultures adopted the old religion of Babel, Nimrod, Semiramis, and Tammuz.

The Hindu trinity's crescent is Shiva, the destroyer. The crescent is part of the AUM symbol and is an ancient venerated artifact. Hinduism perpetuates the worship of the host of heaven, Nimrod's star-worship. This infected the teachings of the Yahudim, as they also began to worship the **host of heaven.**

(See Acts 7:42)

Pagans practice the old religion of Babel, serving Nimrod, Semiramis, and Tammuz in babbled names.

The Hindu trinity reveals Allah as Shiva, the destroyer. Note the crescent and star in the Hindu AUM symbol:

Shiva worship is associated with crescents. The beads and crescents on the Hindu shaman above did not appear out of nowhere, but rather began with the rebellion of Nimrod.

The ancients saw the motion of the stars as they turned around a central point, imitating this with the ritual of circumambulation:

KABA (ABOVE) - **STUPA** (NEXT PAGE)

TIBETAN STUPA

TIBETAN SHIVA SHRINES

SHIVA CRESCENT

TIBETAN STUPA

CIRCUMAMBULATING RITUAL OBJECT

DOMES

The original Tower of Babel may have resembled a domed ziggurat. As the worship of the host of heaven spread on the Earth, Babel's customs and designs did also. Structures or objects within them had sexual overtones to them. The dome feature is shared by both religious and governmental entities in every time and place. In the photo above we see two Shiva shrines with rectangular walls, and a shaft-like object in the center of both. They appear identical to the early photos of the kaba at Makkah. The photo also shows devotees walking around the larger Shiva shrine. The tip of the tall spire has a crescent and star, indicating Shiva and Shakti. These are Hindu shrines, not Islamic, so there can be no doubt that the Kaba at Makkah was originally a Shiva shrine.

Hinduism invaded the Levant (eastern Mediterranean area) like a tidal wave about 200 BCE. It's "enlightenment" was embraced into existing cultures, even Yisharal (Israel).

Ancient tombs took on the architecture of Shiva shrines, having domes designed for them. Herod's tomb was one example.

In architecture around the world, the dome is the male sexual object (Shiva), and the building below is the female (Shakti). The gurus know this, as do the secret societies that build these pagan religious structures around the world.

Buildings such as mosques, Byzantine and Catholic cathedrals, and "capitol" buildings around the world are modelled after Shiva shrines. The dome is Shiva's penis, and the dragon is waving it in everyones' face, including Yahusha's. These things are not accidental, but are by design. The US Capitol building in Washington, DC is called the "temple of Libertas." Libertas is the Roman equivalent to Shakti, or Semiramis of Babel.

PANTHEON
Rome, Italy

SANTA MARIA AD MARTYRES

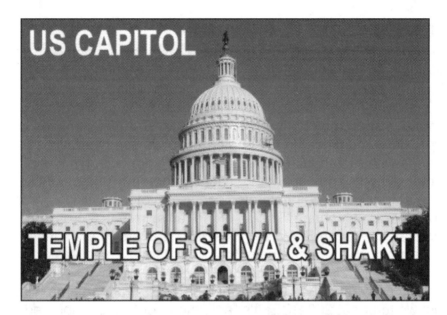

The famous Taj Mahal mimmicks the design of a Shiva temple:

ROMAN BASILICA

HINDU SHIVA SHRINE

A cassock is the long garment worn by clergy, and those who assist in rituals. The Hindu aspect of this garment is striking. The design of a cassock, and other items worn with them such as beads, have been handed-down from eastern sources who practiced the mystical rituals of Hinduism. The ritual garments sometimes leave nothing to the imagination.

MYTH BUSTER

TORAH INSTITUTE

GARMENTS OF CATHOLIC AND MUSLIM CLERICS ARE HINDU

SHIVA PHALLUS

SHIVA TEMPLE

Many Gnostic ideas were carried over from the eastern teachings of Hinduism. Another was the familiar idea of folding the hands in prayer shown in the illustration. It is called **Namaste**, and means *"the spirit in me bows to the spirit in you."* Again we perceive how the spiritual realm is regarded as perfect, and yet we are commanded to not bow to any entity but Yahuah, the Maker of all things visible and invisible.

PAGAN NAMASTE GESTURE

MUTANT SUN WORSHIP

CATHOLIC NUN   BUDDHIST NUN

TORAH INSTITUTE'S TORAHVISION

In the 2nd century BCE, Egyptian worshippers of Serapis were called by the Greek term: *Christians*.

They bowed to crux-shaped objects, the ancient symbol of the Sun. The roots of Christianity originate from Greek Suncults in Egypt, but Constantine formally adopted all the pagan Sun worship together with the Roman Suncult's existing Magisterium. The Roman Kaiser/pope and cardinals' open Sun worship became veiled. Babel's mother of harlots wore the disguise of Christianity as the 4th beast.

A great deal of Babel's Sun worship came through Hinduism, even the "holy waters" of the Ganges was brought over into early Catholicism. The halos on statues was first expressed in Hinduism's idolatry, and adopted by early Catholicism. The prayer beads (repetitive prayers) came into Catholicism later, adopted from Hinduism through Islam at Fatima, a city in Spain captured from the Moors by Catholics.

An apparition of "Mary" handed the beads to several children. Hinduism is prevalent in Islam and Catholicism, and it also affected the followers of Torah as we are about to see.

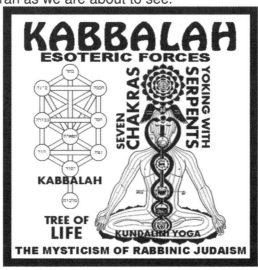

KABBALAH
The Mysticism of Rabbinic Judaism

This subject concerns **teachings**, not people.

When we learn new things concerning our behavior, it's our responsibility to test them with the Word. KABBALAH is the study of how to receive fulfillment. Advocates say it is a secret method to connect to forces to attain fulfillment. Its secrets are intended to be understood only by a small number of people with a specialized knowledge. Kabbalah is a mystical interpretation of inner meanings in the Torah and oral traditions of the fathers.

The study of Kabbalah emerged 700 years after Islam with the publication of the **Zohar**.

ZOHAR

The Zohar is the chief Kabbalah text, which directs Torah study along **4-levels** of interpretation known by the acronym **PaRDeS:**

Parshat (simple, surface meaning)

Remez (hinted)

D'rash (search)

Sud (hidden)

Zohar means splendor, and first appeared in Spain in the 13th century, published by Moses de Leon.

Interest in it exploded during the 16th century through "Rav" Isaac Luria. He promoted the Zohar, echoing Leon's claim that the thoughts were based on the writings of a 1st century "rabbi" Shimon Bar Yochai, under the inspiration of "Elijah" (AliYahu).

Focusing on mystical concepts, Kabbalah reached its height in the later Middle Ages among the Hasidim. It involves esoteric (secret) ciphers (codes), an approach to Scripture directly **condemned by Yahusha in Luke 8**. Kabbalah has evolved into new forms among Christians, New Agers, and occultists.

YOKE OF KABBALAH

The Kabbalist teacher's **YOKE**, or teachings, allows his student access to higher-level interpretations through so-called secret codes. Today we hear about codes being discovered, exploiting the curiosity of allegory-seeking individuals. Tradition is a yoke.

Yahusha contrasted **His yoke** with the yoke of tradition:

"Take My yoke [teaching] **upon you and learn from Me, for I am meek and humble in heart, and you shall find rest for your beings. For My yoke is gentle and My burden is light."**

(Quoted from Mt 11:29, 30)

The Kabbalah student looks upon his teacher as his **exalted one**, thus the title, RABBI, *my exalted one*.

The term **rabbi** is not found in the TaNaK, but the term RAB is, meaning *chief*. Danial was appointed **rab magi** by the king of Babel, meaning chief magician. He was not a practicianer of magic in any way. His behavior led to a conspiracy that led to his being thrown into a den of lions where Yahuah protected him.

Gnosticism (knowledge) is considered vital to enable one to reach awareness, or perfection.

The eastern philosophy of Hinduism teaches a method or path (dharma, path of righteousness) that leads a person out of the karmic cycle of reincarnation, into nirvana (nothingness).

This goal of oblivion is the essence of Eastern philosophy, and the transcendental state is represented by the **sky-blue skin of their many deities**.

As we consider the origins of Kabbalah, we draw parallels everywhere to Hinduism's mystical thought.

The terms Zohar (splendor), Nirvana, enlightenment, connecting (yoking) to forces/energies, the **4-levels of interpretation**, dharma, Rabbi/Guru, and much more indicate there is a direct correlation between Kabbalah and Karmic traditions of Hinduism, by means of a methodical process of learning: aka, Gnosticism.

"Truly, I say to you, whoever does not receive* the reign of Yahuah as a little child, shall certainly not enter into it." Mark 10:15 *(Kabbalah means *receive*)

"'Forsaking the command of Alahim, you hold fast the tradition of men.' And He said to them, 'Well do you set aside the command of Alahim, in order to guard your tradition.'" Mark 7:8, 9

THE YEAST OF THE PHARISEES: RABBINIC JUDAISM

Yahusha was fiercely opposed by men referring to themselves as "rabbis", and He spoke of their knowledge:

"Woe to you learned in the Torah, because you took away the key of knowledge. You did not enter in yourselves, and those who were entering in you hindered." Luke 11:52

Rabbis banned the Name, Yahuah.

The rabbis taught the oral law of the fathers, also referred to as the **traditions of the fathers**. In that day, it was called **"Ioudaismos"**, the religion of the Yahudim. The word **rabbi** is not found in the TaNaK. This sect is known today by its advocates as "Rabbinic Judaism." They were the Pharisees, the "separated ones" who specified teachings. Some believe Rabbinic Judaism to be the Hebrew roots of the faith. Tradition is not our foundation but is the leaven we have to purge.

TRADITIONS OF MY FATHERS
PAUL'S FORMER WAY

"For you have heard of my former way of life in Yahudaism, how intensely I persecuted the body of Alahim, and ravaged it. And I progressed in Yahudaism beyond many of my age in my race, being exceedingly ardent for the traditions of my fathers." Gal 1:13-14

This **YOKE** was not the Torah of Mosheh; it was the *traditions of the fathers.* Now we can understand what this means:

"Now then, why do you try Alahim by putting a yoke on the neck of the taught ones which neither our fathers nor we were able to bear?" Acts 15:10

The **yoke** (teachings) of the traditions of the fathers was keeping men from calling on the Name of Yahuah, and by their **traditions** men were being confused by the wisdom of men, falsely called knowledge. Gnosticism, mystical and allegorical interpretations, were influences originating outside the true faith.

"How is it that you do not understand that I did not speak to you concerning bread, *but* to beware of the leaven of the Pharisees and Sadducees?"

Then they understood that He did not say to beware of the leaven of bread, but of the teaching of the Pharisees and the Sadducees." Mt. 16:11-12

Question: What is the leaven, or yeast of the Pharisees?

Answer: **Rabbinic Judaism, the traditions of the fathers.**

GURU = RABBI

An advocate of Hinduism is trained by their Guru/Yogi-instructor to perform exercises to "yoke" with "life-forces" (**ki**, which are, in truth, spiritual demonic entities). A bond of trust is formed between the teacher and his disciple. A Guru is exactly like a rabbi, guiding the learner. The teacher is referred to as a spiritual master, one who has reached "self-realization" or "fulfillment."

The Guru and the rabbi are the same.

Yoga, a form of Hindu prayer, is an exercise of meditation and astral projection performed by the advocate, called a **yogi**.

The term yoga means to "yoke" and is a union with energies or forces. This is the same goal proposed by Kabbalah, to connect to forces to maintain fulfillment.

The yoga-union with the "forces" proposes to elevate their consciousness to successively higher **chakra**-levels, a **serpent force** in their spine is to guide this process. The goal to achieve is the realization of truth, or perfection. This goal perfectly aligns with Kabbalah, to achieve "fulfillment."

Tantric and Kundalini yoga are the two most popular forms, but all yoga is re-packaged in a variety of ways for consumption in the western world. Today we see Jewish Yoga, Torah Yoga, Holy Yoga, Christian Yoga, Hot Yoga, etc.,.

AWARENESS THROUGH FOUR LEVELS

Interpretation of the eastern texts is guided by Tantric Gurus that control their students with vows of various kinds. They reinforce their control with physical and psychological exercises. Their sacred texts include the **Vedas**, the **Bhagavad Gita**, and **Sruti**. In these sources we discover **Aja**, the *Absolute*, or unborn-eternal consciousness. The self-realized Guru teaches there are four levels of awareness (truth). When we consider all of these elements together, they point to an early interchange between eastern Gnosticism and its influences on **Rabbinic Judaism** (the sect known as Pharisees) from the 1st century forward.

Neither Yahusha nor any of the prophets gave any hint there are four levels of interpreting His inspired Word. Ephesians 4 tells us the gentiles have **darkened minds** filled with ignorance, and they are tossed about by every wind of teaching.

Hinduism has many mystical rabbit trails, and many of them were absorbed into Catholicism such as: beads/rosaries, forehead ashes, haloes, domes, statues, steeples/stupas, holy water (like the Ganges), the gohonzon gold tabernacle, and even the way the folded hands are held palm-to-palm called **Namaste,** all stem from Hinduism. This hand gesture means *"the spirit in me bows to the spirit in you."*

Yahusha instructed us to build upon the Rock, a firm foundation. We see the highest knowledge we can attain is His **Name** and His **Word: "I bow myself toward Your set-apart Hekal, and give thanks to Your Name for Your kindness and for Your truth; for You have made great Your Word, Your Name, above all."** Psalms 138:2

The **Zohar** and **Talmud** did not exist at the time Yahusha warned His Natsarim of the yeast/leaven of the Pharisees.

The **yeast** He spoke of was the **traditions of the fathers**, the oral teachings passed from Rabbi/Guru to student considered to be secret interpretations. **The leaven is Rabbinic Judaism.**

Those who follow the **teachings of the fathers** embodied in the Zohar and Talmud withheld the **Name of Yahuah**, the key of knowledge. The Zohar and Talmud have only held them back, and all those under the influence of men teaching from them.

THE NAME IS STONE THE BUILDERS REJECTED
"The stone which the builders rejected has become the chief corner-stone." Psalms 118:22 (THE NAME IS YAHUAH)

It doesn't require four levels of interpretation to arrive at this Truth. In their pursuit of awareness and enlightenment, their minds have been veiled from understanding, until they receive Yahusha's Spirit to enlighten their hearts - 2Co 3:14-16 tell us:

"But their minds were hardened, for to this day, when the old covenant is being read, that same veil remains, not lifted, because in Mashiak it is taken away. But to this day, when Mosheh is being read, a veil lies on their heart. And when one turns to the Master, the veil is taken away."

CRESCENT
3RD EYE   ASHES
SERPENT
BEADS

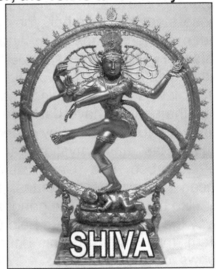

SHIVA

GNOSTICISM INVASION
Beginning around 200 BCE, ideas from the east spread across the entire eastern Mediterranean region, known as the Levant.

The Hindu concept of yin-yang, light/darkness, and material vs. immaterial were the central features of Gnostic teaching.

Everything **physical** was considered imperfect and corrupt, while everything unseen (or spiritual) was perfect. *Rabbinic Judaism* became infused with these ideas as well, and it began to spread among the early **Natsarim**, the first followers of Yahusha.

HINDUISM – MYSTICAL AND SPOOKY

Gnosticism's influence explains why Yahukanon (John) speaks against ideas being spread about Yahusha *not coming in the flesh*, but instead was believed to be an incorporeal being, spirit, apparition, or phantasm.

How could Yahusha be perfect if He took the form of a physical body, if all matter is intrinsically corrupt and defiled?

You can easily see how a person influenced by doctrines of **reincarnation** from Hinduism would be conflicted, since perfection would suggest that nirvana (self-realization) was achieved. The manifestation of a *perfected-being* was expected to be incorporeal, without material substance. Yahukanon (John) was dealing with this divisive and demonic error head on:

"By this you know the Ruach of Alahim: Every ruach that confesses that Yahusha Mashiak has come in the flesh is of Alahim, and every ruach that does not confess that Yahusha Mashiak has come in the flesh is not of Alahim. And this is the ruach of the anti-mashiak which you heard is coming, and now is already in the world." 1Yn 4:2, 3

Paul had to deal with the mystics as well, as he dismantled the Hindu teachings of **asceticism** - consider Col 2:20-23:

"If, then, you died with Mashiak from the elementary things of the world, why, as though living in the world, do you subject yourselves to regulations: 'Do not touch, do not taste, do not handle' – which are all to perish with use – according to the commands and teachings of men? These indeed have an appearance of wisdom in self-imposed worship, humiliation and harsh treatment of the body – are of no value at all, only for satisfaction of the flesh."

New winds of doctrine are disturbing a number of Natsarim today. The **knowledge of Torah** is the only way to reach the goal: **LOVE**. Knowledge for the sake of knowledge will not help us learn how to love, we bear the fruits of the Ruach of Yahusha by obeying Him. The knowledge of Torah is what is forgotten:

"My people have perished for lack of knowledge. Because you have rejected knowledge, I reject you from being priest for Me. Since you have forgotten the Torah of your Alahim, I also forget your children." Hos 4:6

To prepare for the Day of Yahuah (the return of Yahusha) we do not need the Zohar: **"Remember the Torah of Mosheh, My servant, which I commanded him in Horeb for all Yisharal– laws and right-rulings. See, I am sending you Aliyahu the** prophet before the coming of the great and awesome day of Yahuah. And he shall turn the hearts of the fathers to the children, and the hearts of the children to their fathers, lest I come and smite the Earth with utter destruction." Mal 4:4-6

There is no mention in the inspired Word of Yahuah about a Zohar, a Talmud, or *levels of interpretation*. Tradition claims that Mosheh transmitted oral teachings, later perceived as secrets, but this is untrue. All the Words of Yahuah were **read** aloud. They weren't oral and passed down by memorization.
- See Dt. 27:3, 2 Kings 23:2, 2 Kron. 34:30

Danial had no need for a Zohar, and that's a good thing, because it was not coming for another 1900 years.

Yekezqel (Ezekiel) chapter 8 describes the mixture of Babel's **Zodiac** (animal figures) on the inside walls of Yahuah's Temple. **We are His Temple now, made without hands.**

Hot yoga or Kabbalah has no place in His Temple, nor does the Zodiac. In the ruins of several ancient synagogues we find the floor mosaics depicting the signs of the zodiac.

Where did Yahuah command such a thing?

Stephen exposed the worship of the **host of Heaven** (Acts 7:42) in his day, and even in our time the traditions of the fathers continue to lead hearts into futility.

The *KJV* translates Hebrew words based on what they knew of the heavens, which over 400 years ago was limited to the *Babylonian zodiac*. Galaxies were not discovered or imagined until the 1930's, and yet Yahuah had Hebrew words for them in the book of Ayub (Job). As for pagan ideas infused earlier by Jerome, there is no word **cross** in Hebrew or Greek, so the KJV followed the **Latin Vulgate of Jerome**. He inserted "crux" when he could have used the Latin word *stauro* for the Greek word *stauros* – a pole or stake. Human traditions remain for centuries or even millennia if not corrected. We must be vigilant and guard the **Name** and the **Word;** nothing is to be added or taken away.

If we can get past all the manmade *wormwood*, yeast, and old wine, our older brothers in the faith have preserved the Living Words. If only they had not mixed things up with human ideas.

Natsarim are falling into men's teachings at an alarming rate; it's as if they will believe anything that someone dreams up.

It's getting so delusional, someone may come along to explain how Tarot cards might help divine the future return of Yahusha, or **blood-moon tetrads** – oops, too late; *been there, did that.*

Yahusha said we would not know the day or the hour, but **we will know the season**. The Day of Yahuah will snap closed at the time of the harvest, in the 7th moon one of these years.

Yahusha would not consult the zodiac, or infer there are **codes** concealed in Scripture to be understood only by a small number of people with specialized knowledge. What He said, He said to all: "**watch**". Yahuah has not spoken in secret:

"'**Come near to Me, hear this: I have not spoken in secret from the beginning; from the time that it was, I was there.**

And now the Master Yahuah has sent Me, and His Spirit.'

Thus said Yahuah, your Redeemer, the Set-apart One of Yisharal, 'I am Yahuah your Alahim, teaching you what is best, leading you by the way you should go. If only you had listened to My commands! Then your peace would have been like a river, and your righteousness like the waves of the sea." YashaYahu / Isaiah 48:16-18

MattithYahu chapter 23 gives us Yahusha's perspective on men's traditions. It's silly to think Yahusha likes the Zohar, the Talmud, the zodiac, or is pleased when people are taught about *secret codes* hidden in His Word.

Take on Yahusha's yoke (teachings), and learn from Him.

Other yokes can get more involved with snakes:

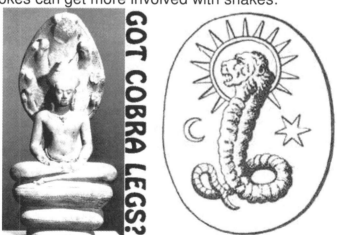

SERPENT COILS, CHAKRAS, ENERGY VORTEXES?

This Sanskrit word *chakra* produces the Greek word KUKLOS, meaning wheel, circle, or coil. In Pagan rituals people often assembled in circular patterns to perform rituals.

In Hinduism, the circular arrangement represents the cycle of rebirth. The 7 chakras in the spine to the head are imaginary vortexes of energy centers for **ki**, the life force (serpent power).

By relaxing and opening to the "forces" a yogi (practitioner of yoga) may become possessed by fallen malakim, coming under the control of one or several demonic entities. Gem-tipped wands, Tarot cards, magic chants, 3rd eye training, crystals, paranormal contact, trances, drug sorcery, pixie dust, scrying, tossing chicken bones, and reading auras are facilities that open a person to demonic possession.

Scripture refers to these things as wickedness.

Teach Truth, not wickedness; rebellion is as witchcraft.

Listen to no teaching authorities other than Yahusha.

RANDOM COINCIDENCE?

There's an incredible amount of **witchcraft** practiced openly which few people perceive as evil in Yahusha's eyes. Instead of pledging ourselves to invisible genies, wearing wizard caps, baking cakes for the queen of heaven, lighting candles and making wishes, we need to be restored to favor with Yahusha.

Paganism is as paganism does. If we practice evil things, we will be barred from the presence of Yahusha, and not be allowed to enter through the gates of the New Yerushalayim.

"Blessed are those doing His commands, so that the authority shall be theirs unto the tree of life, and to enter through the gates into the city. But outside are the dogs and those who enchant

with drugs, and those who whore, and the murderers, and the idolaters, and all who love and do falsehood." – Rev 22:14-15

Why should we avoid Nimrod's star-worship? Because . . .

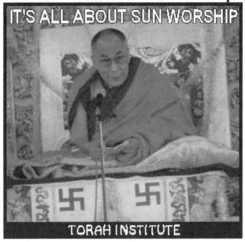

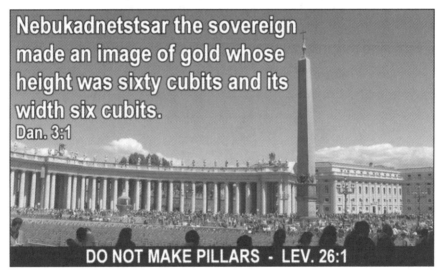

A day is coming, burning like a furnace, when Yahuah will end the reign of Babel and set up His eternal kingdom. 2Pet 3:10-12

FOR THE UNPREPARED, THE TERROR WILL BE UNBELIEVABLE

SHINTO SHOWS ITS SHIVA

What has been concealed will be revealed (Mt. 10:26).
Pagan shrines are only about one thing: sexual fertility.
On the first Sunday of April in Kawasaki, Japan, Shinto priests officiate in a festival called Kanamara Matsuri, or penis festival.

At least 95% of the population is Shinto or Buddhist, and they view their behavior as completely normal. Instead of feeling shame, they are profoundly gleeful about their behavior. With the same kind of warm-hearted fervor the western world embraces Christmas and Santa Claus (who is vicariously Nimrod), the Japanese culture celebrates sex. Giant penises and vaginas are paraded through the streets and around the Shinto shrines. The western mind is appalled at such open debauchery, yet they fail to see how they do the same thing with the Christmas tree, ornaments, tinsel, and wreaths. These are the western versions of penises, testicles, semen (tinsel, and rice at weddings), and vagina-wreaths everywhere. Yahuah ordered us to never bring such abominations into our homes (Dt. 7:25-26). December 25th was originally the time of the rebirth of all solar deities, the **nativity** of the Sun. Nimrod was worshipped as the Sun, which is why we see his ancient figure we now call "Santa" flying all around at this time of year. Nimrod is the first "super-man" to be deified, and became every solar deity from Krishna, Molok, to Constantine's Apollo. Our guilt remains since we claim we see.

UNCOVERING THE NAKEDNESS; THE BALLS (TESTICLES), TINSEL (SEMEN), AND RIBBONS (HYMEN)

THE ERECT POLE, HAT, TREE, OR SPIRE ARE HIDDEN SYMBOLS OF MALE FERTILITY
THE PHALLUS, AND THE ACCOMPANYING VAGINA, THE WREATH, ARE DETESTABLE

"So this I say, and witness in the Master, that you should no longer walk as the gentiles walk, in the futility of their mind, having been darkened in their understanding, having been estranged from the life of Alahim because of the ignorance that is in them, because of the hardness of their heart, who, having become callous, have given themselves up to indecency, to work all uncleanness with greediness."
- Ephesians 4:17-19

What Does Paganism Look Like?

Pagan behavior is the obstacle we read about in Scripture that Yahuah was constantly warning us to avoid. The world is filled with the behavior. Tradition makes the paganism appear to be acceptable to all because it is a part of most people's lifestyle.

Most often it is perceived to be secular, yet the source of the behavior can be easily traced to ancient pagan rituals.

To celebrate a **birthday** is a fine example of what paganism looks like. The first birthday was celebrated for Nimrod as the Sun deity. Nimrod's birthday was at the solstice, and Santa, Molok, Apollo, Shammash, Mithras, and all other Sun deities are vicars of Nimrod. The cone hats, candles, cake, making a wish, and receiving presents borrowed directly from witchcraft, and the worship of the host of heaven.

The birthday is the most important day to a witch.

DID YAHUSHA CELEBRATE HIS BIRTHDAY?

There was an observance in the winter that Yahusha attended, but it was in remembrance of overthrowing Greek tyrants. Hanukkah at Yahukanon 10:22 is seen in most translations as "Feast of the Dedication." This shows that Yahusha was observing **Hanukkah** with His culture around Him as a national celebration for the victory over the Greek tyranny of Antiochus Epiphanes in 165 BCE. Although well into the winter time, there is no mention of Yahusha's birthday at Jn. 10. Yahusha was very much involved with Hanukkah, but not His birthday. The pharaoh of Egypt and Herod celebrated their birthdays (as Scripture informs us), and someone died at both events. Scripture doesn't encourage Yahuah's people to have any part in birthdays; they are the foundation of astrology.

Paganism - what does it look like? Trees, boughs of greenery, wreaths, fertility symbols (eggs, rabbits), pillars (steeples), bowing or kneeling to statues, praying to the dead (ancestors or "saints"), rosaries, using "holy" water (as the Hindu practice of splashing water of the Ganges River), and many other things that would shock the unprepared person.

SYNCRETISM

The 19th century philosopher and theologian Soren Kierkegaard wrote in his book, *Purity Of Heart*:

". . .the larger the crowd, the more probable that that which it praises is **folly**, and the more improbable that it is **truth**; and the most improbable of all that it is any **eternal truth**."

Occult hierarchies have led mankind into great darkness through the blending of pagan traditions.

Syncretism is making stuff mean other stuff. The world is so vast, there was little chance anyone would recognize similarities in the symbols and behavior of two remote cultures. As more people began to migrate to distant continents the symbol of the cross was found to be the most common ancient solar icon. It was found everywhere, and was worshipped from the very beginning with the "reincarnation" of Nimrod as Tammuz. Add the babbling that resulted from the Tower of Babel, and people carried the pagan practices far and wide. The Egyptians worshipped the host of heaven with fertility, and illustrated a great deal of Nimrod's-star worship on walls. Here is the sky deity Nut:

PHILOSOPHY OF MEN – THE GREAT DANGER

"Let no one deceive you with empty words, for because of these the wrath of Yahuah comes upon the sons of disobedience. Therefore do not become partakers with them. For you were once darkness, but now you are light in the Master. Walk as children of light – for the fruit of the Ruach is in all goodness, and uprightness, and truth – proving what is well-pleasing to the Master. And have no fellowship with the fruitless works of darkness, but rather expose them. For it is a shame even to speak of what is done by them in secret. But all things being exposed are manifested by the light, for whatever is manifested is light." Eph. 5:6-13

Exposing mythology and false ideas that billions of people sincerely believe will make enemies, even though the Truth is shared out of love. They would rather keep doing the error than change, because everyone around them will think something strange has happened to them.

"So then, have I become your enemy, speaking truth to you?" Gal. 4:16

"Therefore, since Mashiak suffered in the flesh, arm yourselves also with the same mind, because he who has suffered in the flesh has ceased from sin, so that he no longer lives the rest of his time in the flesh for the lusts of men, but according to the desire of Alahim. For we have spent enough of our past lifetime in doing the desire of the nations, having walked in indecencies, lusts, drunkenness, orgies, wild parties, and abominable idolatries, in which they are surprised that you do not run with them in the same flood of loose behaviour, blaspheming, who shall give an account to Him who is ready to judge the living and the dead." 1 Pet 4:1-5

Gentile cultures have inherited only lies, and have turned aside to myths. Winston Churchill once remarked that once in a while we will stumble over the Truth, but most people simply get up and brush themselves off, and carry on as if nothing happened.

 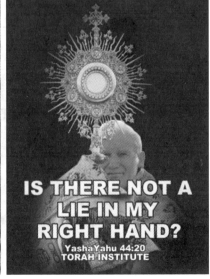

HOW MUCH NONSENSE DOES IT TAKE TO WAKE US UP?

Our capacity to believe lies is limitless. The only thing that can break through the trance (or spell) that is deceiving us is Truth:

"So Yahusha said to those Yahudim who believed Him, 'If you stay in My Word, you are truly My pupils, and you shall know the Truth, and the Truth shall make you free.'" Yn. 8:31-32

"Remember the Torah of Mosheh"
The message of AliYahu for the last days
(See Mal. 4:1-6)
The Ten Commandments teach us how to love Yahuah, and love one another.
We are to do to others as we would have them do to us.

SATI: PRACTICE OF WIDOW BURNING

The Hindu practice of widow-burning is an old tradition in India. Upon the death of a devotee of Shiva, a man's widow is placed alive on the pyre of her husband, often involuntarily. This tradition also originates from the worship of Shiva. In this mythology (yet sincerely believed), Sati is a reincarnation of Shakti, Shiva's wife. The perverseness of all the details of the things said and done concerning Shiva and his wife are abhorrent in the extreme. Suffice it to say, it is shameful even to mention the things pagans are involved in.

Yahuah was so angry over the behavior of pagans He ordered His people to wipe out every trace of their existence under the guidance of Mosheh's successor, Yahusha (Joshua).

In another book in this series, the REAPERS, the order of events on and around the Day of Yahuah are brought into focus. Yahuah will remove all things offensive from the whole Earth.

The Vatican has inherited no small measure of Nimrod's rebellion.
Lev. 26:1 tells us to never erect any pillars in our land, so instead of listening to Yahuah, we erect steeples, minarets, spires, stupas, obelisks, everywhere.

EGG-SHAPED

PHALLIC OBELISK FROM EGYPT IN CENTER OF OVATO TONDO

The shape of the oval space above mimmicks the shape of the Hindu ritual object called the yoni (Shakti) into which the male object (Shiva) is inserted.

The Egyptian stone obelisk completes the Shivalingam.

"The heart is crooked above all,
and desperately sick – who shall know it?" YirmeYahu 17:9

TORAH OF ᴙYƎⱿ
COVENANT OF KINDNESS
TEACHING HOW TO LOVE

1. I AM YAHUAH YOUR ALAHIM
   HAVE NO OTHER BEFORE MY FACE

2. YOU DO NOT BOW TO IMAGES

3. YOU DO NOT CAST THE NAME OF
   YAHUAH YOUR ALAHIM TO RUIN

4. REMEMBER SHABATH
   TO KEEP IT QODESH

5. RESPECT YOUR FATHER
   AND YOUR MOTHER

6. YOU DO NOT MURDER

7. YOU DO NOT BREAK WEDLOCK

8. YOU DO NOT STEAL

9. YOU DO NOT BEAR FALSE
   WITNESS AGAINST YOUR NEIGHBOR

10. YOU DO NOT COVET YOUR
    NEIGHBOR'S WIFE, HOUSE, FIELD,
    SERVANTS, ANIMALS, OR ANYTHING
    BELONGING TO YOUR NEIGHBOR

LOVE ONE ANOTHER
AS I HAVE LOVED YOU

LOVE YAHUAH, LOVE YOUR NEIGHBOR

For more books by this author:
torahzone.net
yahusha.net